STRIKE IT LUCKY QUIZ BOOK

Cheryl Brown

BOXTREE

First published in Great Britain 1992 by Boxtree Ltd

STRIKE IT LUCKY is produced by Thames Television Plc in association with Blair Entertainment/Kline & Friends and Talbot Television

Author: Cheryl Brown
Designer: Anita Ruddell
Typesetter: DP Photosetting
Printed and bound in Great Britain
by Cox & Wyman Ltd
Reading, Berkshire

For Boxtree Limited
Broadwall House
21 Broadwall
London
SE1 9PL

Cover design: Anita Ruddell

A CIP catalogue entry for this book is available from
The British Library

ISBN 1 85283 735 7

Contents

Introduction

Thames Television's *Strike It Lucky*, hosted by Michael Barrymore, is one of television's most popular game shows. Similar-type questions as those appearing on the show have been reproduced in this book so that you too can play at home with the *Strike It Lucky Quiz Book*. Whether you choose to play by yourself, against a friend or in a team, you're guaranteed hours of fun and you'll be sure to learn a few things along the way. Advice on how to play and score appears at the beginning of each of the three rounds. Good luck!

Round One

MATCH-UPS

This introductory round will help to limber you up for tougher games to come. In each quiz all the facts you need to gain a maximum score are there in front of you – the tricky part comes in matching the information correctly.

How to score: Score one point for each correct answer; match all ten correctly and gain an extra five points, bringing your maximum tally for each quiz in this round to 15 points.

For added interest: Decide before you begin each quiz how many match-ups you will correctly pair, starting with a minimum of five, and score as follows:

5 pairs = 5 points; 6 pairs = 10 points;
7 pairs = 15 points; 8 pairs = 20 points;
9 pairs = 25 points; 10 pairs = 30 points.

But fail to match the number of pairs you have nominated and pay the hot spot penalty – no points gained for the quiz at all!

Star Turns

Many famous celebrities in the music world were born with names that were destined never to top the bill – because they changed them! Can you match the stars on the right with their real names on the left?

1	Annie Mae Bullock	**A**	Billie Holliday
2	Vincent Craddock	**B**	Ringo Starr
3	Richard Starkey	**C**	Cliff Richard
4	Arnold Dorsey	**D**	Bob Dylan
5	Marie Laurie	**E**	Tina Turner
6	Gordon Sumner	**F**	Elton John
7	Harry Webb	**G**	Engelbert Humperdinck
8	Elenora Fagan	**H**	Lulu
9	Robert Zimmerman	**I**	Gene Vincent
10	Reginald Dwight	**J**	Sting

Answers on page 85.

Cities of the World

Can you match the cities at the bottom of the page with the brief descriptions of them given below?

1 Australia's largest city which was originally founded as a penal colony.

2 A capital city named after Nike, the Greek goddess of victory.

3 A modern capital, designed in the shape of an aeroplane.

4 An April trade fair, Leonardo da Vinci's *Last Supper* and La Scala Opera House are just some of this city's many attractions.

5 Nicknamed the Motor Town, this city is the home of 'Motown' music.

6 Australia's former capital, until Canberra took over that role in 1913.

7 This Windy City, situated on the shores of Lake Michigan, is 'my kind of town . . .'

8 Nicknamed 'Venice of the North', this beautifully preserved medieval city is famous for its lace.

9 Close to Mount Vesuvius and the ruins of Pompeii, this city sustained severe damage from an earthquake in 1980.

10 Ironically this legislative capital has the highest murder rate in the world.

A Milan
B Melbourne
C Bruges
D Nicosia
E Naples
F Brasilia
G Cape Town
H Sydney
I Chicago
J Detroit

Answers on page 85.

An Inventive Mind

Can you match the inventors on the left with the inventions listed on the right?

1	Gottlieb Daimler	**A**	Long-playing record
2	Benjamin Franklin	**B**	Safety pin
3	Alexander Graham Bell	**C**	Printing press
4	Thomas Edison	**D**	Petrol-driven car
5	Dr Peter Goldmark	**E**	Zip fastener
6	Lumière Brothers	**F**	Motor-cycle
7	Johann Gutenberg	**G**	Electric lamp
8	Karl Benz	**H**	Cinema
9	Whitcomb L. Judson	**I**	Lightning conductor
10	Walter Hunt	**J**	Microphone

Answers on page 85.

In Which Year? A Time of Peace

Can you match the main events of the two decades between the First and Second World Wars with the exact year in which they happened?

1 End of Spanish Civil War; Pan-American launches first regular passenger air service across Atlantic; *Wizard of Oz* released.

2 F.D. Roosevelt elected president of the USA; Amelia Earhart first woman to fly solo across the Atlantic.

3 Pharaoh Tutankhamen's tomb found; war ends between Turkey and Greece; James Joyce's novel *Ulysses* published.

4 Charles Lindbergh becomes first person to fly Atlantic solo; first talking picture *The Jazz Singer* released.

5 Accession of King Edward VIII; outbreak of Spanish Civil War; Volkswagen launched in Germany.

6 Hitler becomes Chancellor of Germany; Fred Perry first Britain to win US Tennis Open for 30 years; prohibition repealed in USA.

7 Nine-day General Strike in Britain; Princess Elizabeth born; J.L. Baird gives first demonstration of television.

8 Wall Street Crash; Fleming announces discovery of penicillin; St Valentine's Day gangster massacre.

9 Duke of Windsor marries Mrs Simpson; Chamberlain becomes British prime minister on resignation of Baldwin; Picasso paints *Guernica* to commemorate bombing of Spanish village by German planes that year.

10 Death of Lenin; first Winter Olympics takes place; Ramsay MacDonald becomes first Labour prime minister of Britain.

A 1933
B 1927
C 1937
D 1929
E 1924
F 1939
G 1932
H 1936
I 1926
J 1922

Answers on page 85.

Don't Be Afraid!

A phobia is an overwhelming and often completely irrational fear of something, and there is a seemingly endless list of words for describing the nature of these fears. Pity the person who is pantophobic for they are afraid of everything; now can you identify the ten phobias given below?

1	Claustrophobia	**A**	Spiders
2	Astraphobia	**B**	Marriage
3	Xenophobia	**C**	Fire
4	Bibliophobia	**D**	Thunder and lightning
5	Hydrophobia	**E**	Number 13
6	Ergophobia	**F**	Foreigners
7	Pyrophobia	**G**	Enclosed places
8	Triskaidekaphobia	**H**	Books
9	Arachnophobia	**I**	Work
10	Gamophobia	**J**	Water

Answers on page 85.

Ten Detectives in Search of an Author

At the top of the opposite page, listed on the left are ten fictional detectives; can you match them with their creators listed on the right?

1	Father Brown	**A**	Sir Arthur Conan Doyle
2	Lord Peter Wimsey	**B**	Leslie Charteris
3	Sherlock Holmes	**C**	Georges Simenon
4	Philip Marlowe	**D**	Chester Gould
5	Jane Marple	**E**	Dorothy Sayers
6	Dick Tracy	**F**	Mickey Spillane
7	Simon Templar	**G**	Raymond Chandler
8	Sam Spade	**H**	G.K. Chesterton
9	Inspector Maigret	**I**	Agatha Christie
10	Mike Hammer	**J**	Dashiel Hammett

Answers on page 85.

God Save Them

Can you match the ten descriptions of English and British monarchs given here to the royal personages named at the bottom of this quiz?

1 It is said of him that 'he never said a foolish thing and never did a wise one'.

2 This English king laid claim to the French throne, leading the English forces to victory at the Battle of Agincourt.

3 This warrior king, known by the nickname 'Coeur de Lion', spent only a few months of his ten-year reign in England.

4 Daughter of Henry VIII and Catherine of Aragon, her reign was dominated by her religious fervour.

5 A British king who could not speak English and who spent more time in Hanover than in England. Sir Robert Walpole became England's first prime minister during his reign.

6 The son of the Black Prince, this king was overthrown by

Henry Bolingbroke and left to starve to death in Pontefract Castle.

7 Renounced his throne to marry a divorcee.

8 The youngest surviving daughter of Henry VIII, she never married and was nicknamed 'the Virgin Queen'.

9 This twelve-year-old boy reigned for only two months before being sent to the Tower of London with his younger brother.

10 The first Lancastrian king whose reign was marked by rebellions including that of Owen Glendower in Wales.

A Mary I
B Edward V
C Richard II
D Richard I
E George I
F Henry IV
G Henry V
H Charles I
I Elizabeth I
J Edward VIII

Answers on page 85.

Sporting Winners

The right-hand column below shows ten trophies awarded in the sports listed on the left. Can you match them correctly?

1 Rowing
2 Cricket
3 Soccer
4 Showjumping
5 Rugby Union
6 Rugby League
7 Bowls
8 Tennis
9 Gaelic Football
10 American Football

A Vincent Lombardi Trophy
B Sam McGuire Trophy
C Bowring Bowl
D Davis Cup
E The Ashes
F King George V Gold Cup
G Jules Rimet Trophy
H Courtney Trophy
I Waterloo Cup
J Britannia Cup

Answers on page 85.

Philosophically Speaking

Can you match these profound statements with the philosophers who said them?

1 'I think, therefore I am.'

2 'Man is born free, but everywhere he is in chains.'

3 'I teach you the Superman. Man is something to be surpassed.'

4 'Religion is the opium of the people.'

5 'The life of man (in a state of nature) is solitary, poor, nasty, brutish, and short.'

6 'The unexamined life is not worth living.'

7 'I disapprove of what you say, but I will defend to the death your right to say it.'

8 'Man is by nature a political animal.'

9 'Even while they teach, men learn.'

10 'Happiness is not an ideal of reason but of imagination.'

A Aristotle
B Thomas Hobbes
C Immanuel Kant
D Voltaire
E René Descartes
F Seneca
G Friedrich Nietzsche
H Karl Marx
I Jean-Jacques Rousseau
J Socrates

Answers on page 85.

In Which Year? Fifties/Sixties

Can you match the main events listed below with the years in which they occurred?

1 Winston Churchill leads Conservative party to power; Festival of Britain takes place; *The Archers* radio series begins.

2 John F. Kennedy elected president of the USA; Sharpeville massacre in South Africa – 67 killed by police forces; first episode of *Coronation Street* screened.

3 British H-bomb tested at Christmas Island; USSR launch first satellite, *Sputnik 1*, into space; Anthony Eden, British prime minister, resigns over Suez Crisis.

4 *Apollo 11* space mission successfully puts man on Moon for first time; Richard Nixon becomes president of USA; investiture of Prince of Wales.

5 Beatles release first single; Cuban missile crisis; *Private Eye* magazine launched.

6 Ruth Ellis last woman to be hanged in Britain; first ITV television broadcast; *Rock Around the Clock*, starring Bill Haley, released.

7 Common Market formed; first traffic wardens and parking meters introduced onto London's streets; seven Manchester United football players killed in Munich air crash.

8 Coronation of Queen Elizabeth II; Hillary and Tensing climb Mt Everest; Ian Fleming publishes first James Bond novel, *Casino Royale*.

9 First heart transplant completed by Dr Christian Barnard; Six-Day War between Egypt and Israel; Che Guevara killed.

10 Assassination of US president, J.F. Kennedy; Great Train Robbery; *Dr Who* makes first appearance on British television screens.

A 1969
B 1955
C 1967
D 1953
E 1951
F 1962
G 1963
H 1960
I 1958
J 1957

Answers on page 85.

Beat the Bard

Here are ten famous quotes from the plays of William Shakespeare. Can you decide from which play listed overleaf each quote comes?

1 'Friends, Romans, countrymen, lend me your ears.'

2 'Once more into the breach dear friends.'

3 'The quality of mercy is not strained.'

4 'A rose by any other name would smell as sweet.'

5 'We are such stuff as dreams are made on.'

6 'All the world's a stage, and all the men and women merely players.'

7 'Now is the winter of our discontent made glorious summer by this son of York.'

8 'Some are born great, some achieve greatness, some have greatness thrust upon them.'

9 'To be or not to be, that is the question.'

10 'O! Beware, my lord, of jealousy; It is the green-ey'd monster which doth mock the meat it feeds on.'

A *Hamlet*
B *The Tempest*
C *Julius Caesar*
D *Othello*
E *Twelfth Night*
F *Romeo and Juliet*
G *Merchant of Venice*
H *Henry V*
I *As You Like It*
J *Richard III*

Answers on page 86.

Famous Last Words

The generally accepted last words of some famous people are given below. Can you match the utterances with their utterers?

1 'Et tu Brute?'

2 'I am just going outside and may be sometime.'

3 'I go from a corruptible to an incorruptible crown.'

4 'Why should I see her, she would only want to give a message to Albert.'

5 'Last words are for fools who haven't said enough.'

6 'If this is dying, I don't think much of it.'

7 I shall hear in Heaven.'

8 'More light.'

9 'Thank God I have done my duty.'

10 'I am dying as I have lived, beyond my means.'

A Admiral Nelson
B Benjamin Disraeli
C Lytton Strachey
D Beethoven
E Julius Caesar
F Oscar Wilde
G Capt. Lawrence Oates
H Charles I
I Karl Marx
J Goethe

Answers on page 86.

Out of Africa

Match the African countries listed overleaf with the brief descriptions of them given below.

1 Formerly Bechuanaland, this country consists mainly of the Kalahari Desert.

2 Kilimanjaro, Africa's highest peak, and the Serengeti National Park are just two of its many tourist attractions.

3 This country was founded by the USA in 1822 as a colony for freed negro slaves.

4 The equator divides this country right through the middle. Nairobi is its capital.

5 An independent state within South Africa, diamonds are this country's most important natural mineral resource.

6 This country's fascinating features include Lake Volta, the world's largest artificial lake, 32,000 chiefs and kings, and no political parties.

7 Previously known as Abyssinia, its capital is Addis Ababa.

8 A narrow strip of land surrounded by Senegal, this is Africa's smallest country, whose economy is based largely on the production of groundnuts.

9 Previously known as Northern Rhodesia, this country was led to independence from the British by Kenneth Kaunda in 1964.

10 The country in the 'Horn of Africa'.

A Lesotho
B Zambia
C Ethiopia
D Somalia
E Tanzania
F Kenya
G Liberia
H Botswana
I Ghana
J Gambia

Answers on page 86.

Pen Names

Authors sometimes publish some or all of their work under a pseudonym. Some famous pen names are given on the left of the page below. Can you match these with their true identities on the right?

1 Currer Bell
2 Mark Twain
3 George Eliot
4 Stendhal
5 George Sand
6 George Orwell
7 Mary Westmacott
8 John le Carré
9 Boz
10 Lewis Carroll

A Eric Arthur Blair
B David Cornwell
C Armandine Dupin
D Charles Dickens
E Charlotte Brontë
F Marie Henri Beyle
G Mary Ann Evans
H Rev. Charles L. Dodgson
I Samuel Langhorne Clemens
J Agatha Christie

Answers on page 86.

Legendary Figures

Can you match the legendary figures from Greek mythology to the descriptions given of them below?

1 An early Greek god condemned to carry the heavens on his shoulders.

2 The son of the god Zeus and a mortal woman, he had a dozen tasks to keep him busy in as many years.

3 This mythical Greek hero killed the bull-headed Minotaur and escaped from the monster's labyrinth.

4 Wife of Zeus, the supreme ruler of gods and men.

5 The goddess of health, from whom we get the English word for cleanliness – hygiene.

6 Son and messenger of the god Zeus, his Roman equivalent is Mercury.

7 Aphrodite, the goddess of love, made this handsome youth fall in love with his own reflection as a punishment for his indifference to others.

8 This Greek hero beheaded the Gorgon Medusa who could turn anyone who looked at her into stone.

9 The boastful Greek peasant girl who was turned into a spider by Athene, goddess of wisdom.

10 The Greek poet and musician who travelled to Hades, the land of the dead, to beg for the return of his dead wife Eurydice.

A Hera
B Hermes
C Orpheus
D Perseus
E Arachne
F Heracles
G Theseus
H Atlas
I Hygieia
J Narcissus

Answers on page 86.

Singalong Time

Hollywood musicals have been responsible for popularising some of our most memorable songs – but just how memorable were the films? Can you match the songs listed below with the films in which they featured?

1 'Oh What a Beautiful Morning'; 'Surrey with the Fringe on Top'; 'Poor Jud is Dead'.

2 'Now You Have Jazz'; 'Who Wants to be a Millionaire'; 'True Love'.

3 'Wandrin' Star'; 'They Call the Wind Maria'; 'I Talk to the Trees'.

4 'Secret Love'; 'The Deadwood Stage'; 'Tis Harry I'm Plannin' to Marry'.

5 'Cheek to Cheek'; 'Isn't This a Lovely Day?'; 'The Piccolino'.

6 'You Can't Get a Man with a Gun'; 'Anything You Can Do I Can Do Better'; 'The Girl that I Marry'.

7 'The Boy Next Door'; 'Trolley Song'; 'Have Yourself a Merry Little Christmas'.

8 'Happy Talk'; 'I'm Gonna Wash that Man Right Outa My Hair'; 'Some Enchanted Evening'.

9 'Bless Your Beautiful Hide'; 'Wonderful, Wonderful Day'; 'Sobbin' Women'.

10 'The Night They Invented Champagne'; 'Thank Heaven for Little Girls'; 'I Remember it Well'.

A *Seven Brides for Seven Brothers*
B *Meet Me in St Louis*
C *Annie Get Your Gun*
D *Oklahoma!*
E *South Pacific*
F *Top Hat*
G *Gigi*
H *Calamity Jane*
I *Paint Your Wagon*
J *High Society*

Answers on page 86.

In Which Year? Seventies/Eighties

Can you match the main events listed below with the years in which they occurred?

1. Iranian embassy siege in London; John Lennon shot dead in New York; Solidarity formed in Poland.
2. Romanian leader Ceausescu overthrown and sentenced to death; *Voyager 2* space probe sends pictures of Neptune back to Earth.
3. Queen Elizabeth II's silver jubilee; British tennis player Virginia Wade wins Wimbledon Women's Singles Championship.
4. Britain, Denmark and Ireland join Common Market; VAT introduced; Yom Kippur War between Israel and Arab states.
5. Chairman Mao dies; James Callaghan takes over from Harold Wilson as British prime minister; USA celebrates its bi-centenary.
6. Amoco Cadiz oil tanker disaster; Polish-born pope John Paul II elected, becoming the first non-Italian pope in 450 years.
7. Argentina invades Falkland Islands; Tudor ship *Mary Rose* raised; Channel Four begins broadcasting.
8. Decimalisation introduced in Britain; Idi Amin takes control in Uganda; Stanley Kubrick's controversial film *Clockwork Orange* released.
9. Gorbachev becomes leader of USSR; first Live Aid concert; Rock Hudson dies of AIDS.

10 Women's peace camps set up at Greenham Common; Prince of Wales marries Lady Diana Spencer; first London marathon held.

A	1973	**F**	1989
B	1978	**G**	1985
C	1971	**H**	1977
D	1981	**I**	1976
E	1982	**J**	1980

Answers on page 86.

Childhood Classics

From which of the children's books listed at the top of the opposite page do these groups of familiar characters come?

1 Anne, Dick, 'George', Julian and Timmy the dog.

2 Eeyore, Kanga, Roo, Piglet and Christopher Robin.

3 White Rabbit, March Hare, Mock Turtle and the Queen of Hearts.

4 Mr Grimes, Tom, Mrs Bedonebyasyoudid, Mother Carey and Miss Ellie.

5 Mr Gruber, Mrs Bird, Aunt Lucy, Judy and Jonathan Brown.

6 Orinoco, Tomsk, Great Uncle Bulgaria and Bungo.

7 Toad, Mole, Water Rat, Badger and Weasel.

8 Arrietty, Pod, Homily and Tom Goodenough.

9 The Lost Boys, the Redskins, Smee and Nana.

10 The Oompa Loompas, Augustus Gloop, Violet Beauregarde and Grandpa Joe.

A *Peter Pan and Wendy* (J.M. Barrie)
B *The Wind in the Willows* (Kenneth Grahame)
C *Charlie and the Chocolate Factory* (Roald Dahl)
D *The Borrowers* (Mary Norton)
E *Alice in Wonderland* (Lewis Carroll)
F *The Famous Five Adventures* (Enid Blyton)
G *Winnie the Pooh* (A.A. Milne)
H *Water Babies* (Charles Kingsley)
I *A Bear Called Paddington* (Michael Bond)
J *The Wombles* (Elizabeth Beresford)

Answers on page 86.

Politically Speaking

Can you match the famous quotes below with the statesmen who gave them voice, listed overleaf?

1 'I have nothing to offer but blood, toil, tears and sweat.'

2 'Ask not what your country can do for you, but what you can do for your country.'

3 'Government of the people, by the people, for the people.'

4 'I have a dream.'

5 'Lies, damned lies and statistics.'

6 'Speak softly and carry a big stick.'

7 'Nothing is certain but death and taxes.'

8 'Peace for our time.'

9 'Politics is the art of the possible.'

10 'It will be years – and not in my time – before a woman will lead the Party and become Prime Minister.'

A	Abraham Lincoln	**F**	President J.F. Kennedy
B	Margaret Thatcher	**G**	Benjamin Disraeli
C	Winston Churchill	**H**	Rab Butler
D	Theodore Roosevelt	**I**	Martin Luther King
E	Neville Chamberlain	**J**	Benjamin Franklin

Answers on page 86.

Star Turns Take Two

Many stars of the big screen were born with names that did not fit well with the image of the glamorous movie star - so they changed them. Can you match the actors and actresses on the right with their original names on the left?

1	Marion Morrison	**A**	Michael Caine
2	Joyce Frankenberg	**B**	Judy Garland
3	Archibald Leach	**C**	John Wayne
4	Norma Jean Baker	**D**	Jane Seymour
5	Dino Crocetti	**E**	James Garner
6	Tula Finklea	**F**	Shirley MacLaine
7	Frances Gumm	**G**	Marilyn Monroe
8	Morris Micklewhite	**H**	Dean Martin
9	James Baumgardner	**I**	Cary Grant
10	Shirley Beaty	**J**	Cyd Charisse

Answers on page 86.

The Day Job

Can you match the authors listed below with the jobs they once held?

1	William Shakespeare	**A**	Customs Controller
2	Kenneth Grahame	**B**	Intelligence Agent
3	F. Scott Fitzgerald	**C**	Lloyd's Bank Employee
4	A.J. Cronin	**D**	Policeman
5	Lewis Carroll	**E**	Hollywood Scriptwriter
6	Ian Fleming	**F**	Q.C. Divorce Barrister
7	George Orwell	**G**	Actor
8	T.S. Eliot	**H**	Inspector of Mines
9	John Mortimer	**I**	Mathematics Lecturer
10	Geoffrey Chaucer	**J**	Secretary to the Bank of England

Answers on page 86.

Olympic Winners

The first modern Olympic Games took place in Athens in 1896 when 311 competitors from 13 countries took part. Held every four years, the Olympic Games has grown to become the world's greatest sporting competition. Highlights of ten Olympic Games are given below. Can you match these with the dates and venues given at the bottom of the quiz?

1 First Olympic village established for duration of games. American Mildred 'Babe' Didrikson wins gold medals for javelin and hurdles, and a silver medal for the high jump.

2 Bob Beamon sets his incredible long-jump world record, leaping 55 cm more than anyone ever had before. Many considered this an unbeatable fluke performance achieved due to the high-altitude conditions of this Olympic venue.

3 Soviet Union makes last-minute announcement that it will not be taking part. British athlete Daley Thompson wins decathlon gold.

4 Britain's 'Chariots of Fire' heroes, Eric Liddell and Harold Abrahams, win gold medals in 400 m and 100 m respectively.

5 Marathon leader Italian Dorand Pietri disqualified when helped over finishing line by race officials.

6 First Olympic torch relayed from Olympia, Greece, to the games creating a ceremonial tradition. Black athlete Jesse Owens of the USA wins four gold medals.

7 Canadian athlete Ben Johnson forfeits his gold medal for the 100 m when he fails a drug test.

8 First and only time one of the Olympic events takes place in a different country from the host nation when the equestrian events are held in Stockholm.

9 Swimmer Mark Spitz of the USA wins record seven gold medals. Arab terrorists invade Olympic village leaving 11 Israeli athletes dead at the end of the siege.

10 Romanian gymnast Nadia Comaneci achieves first ever maximum 10.0 marks. Soviet fencer, Boris Onischenko, found to have tampered with his epée and Soviet team therefore forfeit the gold medal.

A 1984, Los Angeles
B 1908, London
C 1976, Montreal
D 1988, Seoul
E 1956, Melbourne
F 1924, Paris
G 1972, Munich
H 1932, Los Angeles
I 1936, Berlin
J 1968, Mexico City

Answers on page 86.

States of the USA

Can you match the States below with the popular names by which they are affectionately known?

1 Alabama
2 New York
3 Washington
4 California
5 Florida
6 Arizona
7 Texas
8 Mississippi
9 Hawaii
10 Pennsylvania

A Lone Star State
B Magnolia State
C The Aloha State
D Keystone State
E Heart of Dixie
F Empire State
G Sunshine State
H Golden State
I Grand Canyon State
J Evergreen State

Answers on page 86.

Collectively Speaking

Can you match the collective nouns below with the animals they are used to describe?

1	Cluster	**A**	Chickens
2	Flock	**B**	Crows
3	Pride	**C**	Pigs
4	Brood	**D**	Rhinoceroses
5	School	**E**	Frogs
6	Leap	**F**	Cats
7	Drove	**G**	Whales
8	Murder	**H**	Sheep
9	Crash	**I**	Lions
10	Army	**J**	Leopards

Answers on page 86.

Zzzzzzz!

Just in case you were dropping off, here's a quiz to really set you thinking. In this final quiz in Round 1, we have chosen ten definitions for ten words beginning with the final letter of the alphabet – Z. Can you match them?

1	Offspring of male zebra and mare	**A**	Zither
2	Monetary unit of Poland	**B**	Zucchetto
3	Dead person revived by black magic	**C**	Zebu
4	Ecclesiastical skull cap	**D**	Zeotrope
5	US English for courgette	**E**	Zloty
6	A humped domestic ox	**F**	Zany
7	A Marsala-flavoured frothy custard	**G**	Zombie
8	An assistant clown or buffoon	**H**	Zebroid
9	Flat, wooden soundbox with strings	**I**	Zabaglione
10	Invention producing illusory movement	**J**	Zucchini

Answers on page 86.

Round Two

KNOWLEDGE TESTERS

Now it's time to put your general knowledge to the test. First, pick a subject on which you would like to answer questions from the seven listed below:

Art and Literature
Film and Television
Geography
History
The Living World
Science and Technology
Sports

The quizzes in this round are split into three sections depending on their level of difficulty, easy (Easy Starters), medium (Warming Up) or hard (Hot Spot). There are three quizzes in each of the first two sections, but only one Hot Spot quiz which should only be tackled if you're a real expert in the field! In a team competition, the Hot Spot quiz makes an ideal semi-final between contestants to decide who goes through to the final round.

How to Score: In this round the number of points scored for a correct answer depends on the level of difficulty of the quiz.

Easy Starters: Score one point for each correct answer. Score ten correct answers and pick up a bonus five points.
Warming Up: Score three points for each correct answer. Score ten correct answers and pick up a bonus 10 points.
The Hot Spot: Score five points for each correct answer. Score ten correct answers and pick up a bonus 20 points.

Now all that remains is for you to choose your category and level of difficulty and begin. Good luck!

Easy Starters

Art and Literature 1

1 What nationality was the surrealist artist René Magritte?

2 Which sister of a famous Romantic poet wrote the horror story *Frankenstein*?

3 Hans Holbein the Younger was court painter to which English monarch?

4 The Little Mermaid statue in Copenhagen Harbour stands as a memorial to which children's author?

5 By what name is Chopin's Waltz in D flat, No. 1, more popularly known?

6 Which artist painted *The Birth of Venus*?

7 Who was the author of *Brideshead Revisited*?

8 In which country is *Heidi*, by Johanna Spyri, set?

9 Which artist became famous for his paintings of 'match-stick men and matchstick cats and dogs'?

10 Who was the composer of *Rhapsody in Blue*?

Answers on page 87.

Art and Literature 2

1 What are the names of the Darling children in J.M. Barrie's play *Peter Pan*?

2 Against the background of which period of history is Leo Tolstoy's *War and Peace* set?

3 By what name are Richard Wagner's series of four operas – *The Rheinegold*, *The Valkyrie*, *Siegfried* and *The Twilight of the Gods* – collectively known?

4 Who wrote the children's classic *Black Beauty*?

5 Who designed St Paul's Cathedral?

6 In Roald Dahl's children's novel *Charlie and the Chocolate Factory*, what is the name of the factory owner?

7 Which twentieth-century novelist includes the following amongst her work: *The Sea, The Sea*, *An Accidental Man* and *Nuns and Soldiers*?

8 Which of the Brontë sisters wrote *Jane Eyre*?

9 Which artist is famous for his paintings of the Moulin Rouge in Paris?

10 What is the name of Scrooge's clerk in Charles Dickens's *A Christmas Carol*?

Answers on page 87.

Art and Literature 3

1 Who wrote *The Great Gatsby*?

2 What is the name of the short story by Franz Kafka in which a man changes into an insect?

3 In Shakespeare's *A Midsummer Night's Dream*, who is the Queen of the Fairies?

4 What is the name of the bear created by children's writer Michael Bond?

5 In which novel by Charles Dickens do the characters of Pip, Miss Havisham, Estella, and Magwitch feature?

6 Which English artist, famous for his landscapes of Suffolk, painted *The Hay Wain*?

7 Which classical Greek writer produced *The Aeneid*?

8 Which noble English poet was described by one of his mistresses as 'mad, bad and dangerous to know'?

9 Who wrote the children's stories which included *How the Grinch Stole Christmas*, *The Cat in the Hat* and *Green Ham and Eggs*?

10 Who was the author of *The Invisible Man*, *The History of Mr Polly* and *The Time Machine*?

Answers on page 87.

Film and TV 1

1. Who played the part of Alf Garnett's daughter in the television comedy series *Till Death Us Do Part*?
2. What was the title of the thirtieth *Carry On* film made in 1992?
3. What was the name of the character played by Anthony Perkins in Alfred Hitchcock's 1960 thriller *Psycho*?
4. What are the names of Donald Duck's nephews?
5. In which film did Warren Beatty play the part of a Beverly Hills hairdresser?
6. Which television soap opera spawned *The Colbys*?
7. Which film musical, directed by Richard Wise with music and lyrics by Richard Rogers and Oscar Hammerstein, was based on the autobiography of singer Maria Trapp?
8. Which television personality game show, hosted by Michael Aspel, is based on the traditional parlour game charades?
9. Which film actress played the part of Lola Lola in *The Blue Angel*?
10. Who is the chairperson of the National Viewers' and Listeners' Association?

Answers on page 87.

Film and TV 2

1 Who played the part of café owner Rick Blaine in *Casablanca*?

2 In which film do the characters CP30, R2D2 and Obi Ben Kenobi appear?

3 What is the name of the pub in *Emmerdale Farm*?

4 Who wrote the novel on which the 1944 film *The Big Sleep* was based?

5 Who played the part of Glenn Miller in *The Glenn Miller Story*?

6 Which television series featured the characters Jed 'Kid' Curry and Hannibal Heyes?

7 Who are the famous parents of actress Jamie Lee Curtis?

8 On which children's television programme do Zippy, George and Bungo appear?

9 Who is the question-master of *Mastermind*?

10 In the 1983 film *Educating Rita*, which actress played the part of working-class student Rita and which actor the part of her Open University tutor?

Answers on page 87.

Film and TV 3

1 By what name was Walt Disney's cartoon character Mickey Mouse known when he appeared in his first film *Plane Crazy* in 1928?

2 Who played the part of the vigilante Paul Kersey in the *Death Wish* films?

3 What part does actress Julie Goodyear play in *Coronation Street*?

4 What was the name of the devil's son in *The Omen*?

5 What was the name of the department store in which the comedy television series *Are You Being Served* was set?

6 Who wrote the television screenplay *The Boys from the Blackstuff*?

7 Which actor played the part of prizefighter Jake La Motta in Martin Scorsese's film *Raging Bull*?

8 Cathy Gale, Tara King and Emma Peel are all characters from which classic television series?

9 Who were the creators of *Thunderbirds*?

10 What is the sequel to *Till Death Us Do Part* which also stars Warren Mitchell in the lead role?

Answers on page 87.

Geography 1

1 By what name was the country of Zimbabwe formerly known?

2 What does OPEC stand for?

3 Popularly referred to as China's Sorrow, what is the correct name for this river?

4 Between which two European countries is Liechtenstein situated?

5 What is the capital of Norway?

6 What is the name of the canal which runs from Liverpool to London?

7 Which two seas are linked by the Suez Canal?

8 Which is the largest of the Greek Islands?

9 What is the official language of Jersey?

10 What is the name of the Brazilian city overlooked by Sugar Loaf Mountain?

Answers on page 87.

Geography 2

1 What does a red triangle printed on a British Ordnance Survey map indicate?

2 What is the proper name of the range of hills often described as the backbone of England?

3 In which ocean can the Solomon Islands be found?

4 What is the highest mountain in Western Europe?

5 What is the name of the lake in London's Hyde Park?

6 What is the capital of Austria?

7 In which English city is the National Exhibition Centre?

8 What is the ancient country of Persia known as today?

9 What is the smallest independent country in the world?

10 What is the monetary unit of Japan?

Answers on page 88.

Geography 3

1 Greenland is a dependency of which European country?

2 What is an Argentinian cowboy called?

3 Between which two European countries is the principality of Andorra situated?

4 By what name is London's Palace of Westminster better known?

5 Its official name is Confederation Helevetique. By what name is this country more popularly known?

6 What is the capital of Egypt?

7 What is the name of the strait which separates the Isle of Wight from mainland Britain?

8 What are lakes Eerie, Huron, Michigan, Ontario and Superior collectively known as?

9 If you were visiting 'Old Faithful' at Yellowstone Park, Colorado, what would you be looking at?

10 What is the longest river in Scotland?

Answers on page 88.

History 1

1 What was the name of the German airship which caught fire, killing 35 people, in 1937?

2 Who assassinated US president Abraham Lincoln in 1865?

3 What name meaning conquerors was given to the sixteenth-century explorers of the New World?

4 Which battle is depicted in the Bayeux Tapestry?

5 Who was the first man to set foot on the Moon's surface on 21 July 1969?

6 What name is given to the political struggles that took place between England and France from 1337–1453?

7 Under the reign of which English king was the Anglican Church formed?

8 What was the monetary value of the first postage stamp issued in Britain in 1840?

9 Who became the leader of Russia following the death of Lenin in 1924?

10 In which year did the Second World War break out?

Answers on page 88.

History 2

1 Name the US president who was forced to resign as a result of the Watergate Scandal of 1973.

2 What was the name of the English naturalist who outlined his theory of evolution in 1851?

3 What was prohibited by the US Prohibition Act of 1920?

4 In which German city did the war trials of Nazi leaders take place in 1945–6?

5 When exactly was the American Declaration of Independence signed?

6 Who was the leader of the Women's Suffrage Movement?

7 What was the name of the tribe ruled by Attila?

8 What is the name given to the struggle between the descendants of Edward III for the English crown?

9 Which dynasty, established in 1368, ruled China until 1644?

10 Who succeeded Elizabeth I to the throne of England on her death in 1601?

Answers on page 88.

History 3

1 In which year did the Great Fire of London take place?

2 By what name is the Nationalist Socialist German Workers' Party, founded by Hitler in 1919, more commonly known?

3 By what name are the six English labourers known who were sent to penal colonies in Australia in 1834 for trying to set up a trade union?

4 Who succeeded to the throne on the death of Britain's longest-reigning monarch, Queen Victoria, in 1901?

5 During which war were the battles of Verdun, Somme and Passchendaele fought?

6 What was founded at the Paris Conference of 1919 to help preserve world peace?

7 Who set a land speed record of 649 km/h in his car 'Bluebird' in 1964?

8 Where did King John sign the Magna Carta in 1215?

9 How did Marie Antoinette meet her death in 1793?

10 What was the name of the ship in which the Pilgrim Fathers set sail for the New World in 1620?

Answers on page 88.

The Living World 1

1 Which bird lays the biggest eggs?

2 What is the term for a creature that eats both plants and animals?

3 What animal is the symbol for the World Wide Fund for Nature?

4 By what name is wild clematis also known?

5 What type of creature is a marmoset?

6 What is the largest species of penguin?

7 Discovery, Bramley and Worcester Pearmain are all varieties of which fruit?

8 What is the commonest species of wild duck in Britain?

9 The leaves of which plant provide a natural antidote to the sting of the nettle?

10 Tamworth, Wessex saddleback and Vietnamese Pot-bellied are all types of what?

Answers on page 88.

The Living World 2

1 What do the following birds have in common: emus, penguins and kiwis?

2 What is a creature that can live both on land and in water called?

3 Copper, monarch, painted lady and red admiral are all types of what?

4 Which flower is named after naturalist Leonard Fuchs?

5 What is the smallest species of owl called?

6 What type of creature is a guppy?

7 From which plant is the drug cocaine obtained?

8 To what family do spiders belong?

9 Desirée, Maris Piper and King Edward are all varieties of which vegetable?

10 What is a female fox called?

Answers on page 88.

The Living World 3

1 By what name is the Atlantic penguin, extinct since 1844, better known?

2 Blackface, Corriedale and merino are all breeds of what?

3 Originally called the Holy Tree because of a legend that it first sprung up in the footsteps of Jesus Christ, by what name is this plant known today?

4 Name the smallest breed of dog.

5 Cantaloupe, honeydew and casaba are all varieties of which fruit?

6 What type of creature is a gecko?

7 How many eyes does a coconut have?

8 Where is a scorpion's sting located?

9 Catkins are the fruit of which tree?

10 In aborigine the name of this animal means 'no drink'. What is it?

Answers on page 88.

Science and Technology 1

1 What are the fontanelle - the areas on a baby's head where the bone has not yet formed - more commonly known as?

2 Where on your body would you find the Achilles tendon?

3 Who was the first man in space?

4 What is palaeontology the study of?

5 By what name is the disease varicella, in which a rash of red spots appears over the body, more commonly known?

6 How many faces does a cube have?

7 Which part of the body is affected by the disease glaucoma?

8 How many planets orbit the Sun?

9 What is the world's hardest natural substance?

10 What is a person who is trained to take X-rays called?

Answers on page 88.

Science and Technology 2

1 Which organs are responsible for removing waste materials from the blood?

2 What is the world's largest passenger plane?

3 What is a bridge called that is designed to carry water?

4 The backbone or spine is made up of 26 small bones. What are these called?

5 Greek philosopher Aristotle established the belief that everything was made up of a combination of just four elements. What were they?

6 What is a doctor who specialises in the treatment of children called?

7 In 1957 the Soviet Union launched the first man-made object into space. What was it called?

8 In which part of the body can the hypothalamus be found?

9 Victims of an hereditary disease which affects mainly males are sometimes referred to as bleeders. From what condition are they suffering?

10 How many sides does an octagon have?

Answers on page 89.

Science and Technology 3

1 What are scientists who study the stars called?

2 What is the longest bone in the human body?

3 How is the disease Acquired Immune Deficiency Syndrome more briefly referred to?

4 If you went to see a chiropodist, which part of your body would he or she treat?

5 Which is the largest planet in the Solar System?

6 What are aeroplanes that generally have no engines called?

7 What are the remains of collapsed stars called?

8 What name is given to the traditional Chinese treatment of using needles inserted into specified points on the body to treat illnesses?

9 In 1984 Apple Macintosh introduced a movable desktop pointing device to the computer world. What is this commonly called today?

10 On which planet did the space probe *Viking 1* land in 1976?

Answers on page 89.

Sports 1

1 By what name was heavyweight boxer Muhammad Ali known before he changed his name in 1964?

2 What is the home football ground of the Glasgow Rangers?

3 Who became the first man to run a mile in under four minutes in 1954?

4 What is the nickname of Brazilian soccer star Edson Arantes do Nascimento?

5 In which year did the English football team last win the World Cup?

6 Over what period of time is France's Le Mans motor race held?

7 This sport is a combination of cross-country running and map-reading. What is it?

8 Steve Davis, Alex Higgins and Dennis Taylor are all well-known names in which sport?

9 With which athletic event is Britain's Steve Backley associated?

10 Which English football team is nicknamed the Pensioners?

Answers on page 89.

Sports 2

1 What nationality is world champion racing driver Niki Lauda?

2 The straddle, the western roll, the scissors and the Fosbury flop are all techniques used in which sport?

3 In which sport are the Ryder, Walker and Curtis cups played for?

4 Where are the TT Motorcycle Road Races held?

5 Which English football team is nicknamed the Canaries?

6 Which sport is governed by the Harvard rules?

7 In which English city can the Anfield football ground be found?

8 With which sport are the names of Mike Tyson, Joe Frazier and Alan Minter associated?

9 In the game of darts, what is the highest score that can be achieved with one dart?

10 In which month is the horse racing event of Ascot held?

Answers on page 89.

Sports 3

1 Which English football team is based at London's White Hart Lane football ground?

2 With which sport are the Harlem Globetrotters associated?

3 Where were the 1992 Winter Olympics held?

4 With which sport are the names of David Broome, Harvey Smith and Hans Günter-Winkler associated?

5 Which English football team is nicknamed the Saints?

6 In which sport is the Lonsdale Belt awarded?

7 At what ground in England are international rugby union matches held?

8 With which sport are the names of Imran Khan, Graham Gooch and Denis Compton associated?

9 From which card game is contract bridge derived?

10 Which team game begins with a bully off?

Answers on page 89.

Warming Up

Art and Literature 1

1 What artistic movement is Matisse associated with?

2 Name the book by T.S. Eliot on which the Andrew Lloyd Webber/Tim Rice musical *Cats* was based.

3 Who wrote the biographical work *The Life of Samuel Johnson*?

4 In which children's novel does the two-headed animal Pushme-Pullyu appear?

5 Which playwright wrote *Accidental Death of an Anarchist*?

6 Who wrote the opera *Carmen*?

7 What is the occupation of the central character, Humphrey Chimpden Earwicker, in James Joyce's novel *Finnegans Wake*?

8 Who wrote *Gone with the Wind*?

9 In Shakespeare's *Tempest*, what is the name of Prospero's slave?

10 Who wrote *The Sailor Who Fell from Grace with the Sea*?

Answers on page 89.

Art and Literature 2

1 In Charles Dickens's novel *Oliver Twist*, who kills Nancy?

2 What was the title of the sequel novel to Robert Graves's *I, Claudius*?

3 Who was the sculptor of *The Burghers of Calais*?

4 Who wrote an opera based on *Billy Budd* by American novelist Herman Melville?

5 What is the name of Phileas Fogg's valet in Jules Verne's adventure novel *Around the World in Eighty Days*?

6 Who wrote *The History Man*?

7 What are the names of the four sisters in Louisa May Alcott's novel *Little Women*?

8 Which Tom Stoppard play tells the story of two characters from Shakespeare's *Hamlet*?

9 In Puccini's opera *Madame Butterfly*, what is the name of the US naval officer who marries Cio Cio San?

10 Holden Caulfield is the central character of which novel by J.D. Salinger published in 1951?

Answers on page 89.

Art and Literature 3

1 Which of Alan Sillitoe's novels is set in Borstal?

2 What is the name of David Copperfield's aunt in Charles Dickens's novel *The Personal History of David Copperfield*?

3 Who wrote *The Dharma Bums*, *Big Sur* and *On the Road*?

4 By what name is the painting *Arrangement in Grey and Black* by James Whistler better known?

5 What is the occupation of James Dixon, the central character in Kingsley Amis's novel *Lucky Jim*?

6 Who was the composer of *Toccata and Fugue*?

7 In Thomas Mann's novel *Death in Venice*, what does the central character, writer Gustav von Aschenbach, die of?

8 What is the name of Maxim De Winter's family home in Daphne du Maurier's novel *Rebecca*?

9 Which Italian playwright wrote *Six Characters in Search of an Author*?

10 Who wrote *The Amorous Adventures of Moll Flanders*?

Answers on page 89.

Film and TV 1

1 Which 1979 film, directed by Francis Coppola, was based on the novel *Heart of Darkness* by Joseph Conrad?

2 Who played the character of Holly Golightly in *Breakfast at Tiffany's*?

3 What is Popeye's enemy called?

4 *Lou Grant*, *Phyllis* and *Rhoda* were all spin-offs of which television series?

5 Who directed *Alien*?

6 Which film, based on a novel by Muriel Spark, was set in the Marcia Blaine School for Girls?

7 Who was the first Director General of the BBC?

8 Who wrote the book on which the 1939 film *The Wizard of Oz*, starring Judy Garland, was based?

9 What part did actress Violet Carson play in *Coronation Street*?

10 What was the name of the character played by Orson Welles in Carol Reed's *The Third Man*?

Answers on page 90.

Film and TV 2

1 Who was the family friend who seduced Benjamin, played by Dustin Hoffman, in *The Graduate*?

2 Which 1956 film, starring Kenneth More in the lead role, celebrated the life of World War Two flying ace Douglas Bader?

3 Who played the part of the mother in the comedy series *Not in Front of the Children*?

4 Name the 1988 David Cronenberg film in which Jeremy Irons played the parts of twin gynaecologists?

5 Which cartoon character was accused of immorality in the Thirties?

6 Oliver Stone's Oscar-winning film *Platoon* is an autobiographical study of infantry life during which war?

7 What is the name of the butler in *The Addams Family*?

8 Who do *Candid Camera*, *Celebrity Squares*, and *$64,000 Question* have in common?

9 What was the title of the 1980 film biography of country and western singer Loretta Lynn, starring Sissy Spacek in the lead role?

10 In which European city is *Don't Look Now*, starring Donald Sutherland and Julie Christie, mainly set?

Answers on page 90.

Film and TV 3

1 In the television comedy series *The Good Life*, who were the Goods' neighbours, played by Paul Eddington and Penelope Keith?

2 In *The Return of the Saint* who played the part of Simon Templar?

3 Who played the part of Judy Garland's husband in the 1954 version of *A Star is Born*?

4 In which fictional town was the *Crossroads* motel located?

5 In the 1938 comedy film *Bringing Up Baby*, starring Cary Grant and Katharine Hepburn, what was unusual about the baby?

6 What is the name of the Boston hospital featured in the US drama series *St Elsewhere*?

7 Which country and western singer starred in the 1980 comedy film *Nine to Five*?

8 Name the duo responsible for creating television's successful satirical puppet show *Spitting Image*?

9 In *Happy Days*, what is the full name of the character 'The Fonz' played by Henry Winkler?

10 Which actor played the part of an English aristocrat, captured by the Sioux, who eventually becomes their leader, in the 1970 film *A Man Called Horse*?

Answers on page 90.

Geography 1

1 In which country is the River Kwai?

2 What is the capital of the People's Republic of Congo?

3 What is the name of the river that flows through the Grand Canyon, USA?

4 Minorca, Majorca and Ibiza belong to which group of islands?

5 Where in the world is Tierra del Fuego?

6 Near to which city do the White Nile and the Blue Nile meet?

7 What is the capital of Bulgaria?

8 On which river does the city of Amsterdam lie?

9 Which city is nicknamed the 'Pearl of the Desert'?

10 What is the state capital of California?

Answers on page 90.

Geography 2

1 What is the national symbol of India?

2 Netherlands and Luxembourg are two of the Benelux countries. What is the third?

3 What is the capital of Malta?

4 What is the name of the strait separating New Zealand's North and South islands?

5 Name the world's northernmost and southernmost capitals.

6 What is Italy's longest river?

7 In which English county are the Quantock Hills?

8 What is the capital of Luxembourg?

9 Which three countries border Paraguay?

10 Granta was the Roman name of which English city?

Answers on page 90.

Geography 3

1 Of which country is Victoria the capital?

2 Where is Montego Bay?

3 What is a drumlin?

4 Between which two countries does the Bay of Bengal lie?

5 On which river does the city of Florence stand?

6 Where are the Tivoli Gardens?

7 In which country is Sinhala spoken?

8 What is the term for a narrow strip of land connecting two larger land areas?

9 What is the capital of Nigeria?

10 The East is known as the Orient; what is the West referred to as?

Answers on page 90.

History 1

1 The Colossus of Rhodes, one of the Seven Wonders of the Ancient World, was a huge bronze statue of a Greek god – which one?

2 Who was the president of the Confederate States of America during the American Civil War?

3 Who became the first British woman MP to take her seat in the House of Commons in 1919?

4 Where did the aborted invasion of Cuba by US forces take place in 1961?

5 Who was the first king of the Tudor dynasty?

6 The Treaty of Westphalia (1648) ended which war?

7 Who was condemned as a heretic at the Diet of Worms in 1521?

8 In which year did the English Civil War begin?

9 Who led the rebellious North American settlers to defeat British troops at the Battle of Lexington in 1775?

10 The Alma, Inkerman, Sevastopol and Balaclava were all battles fought during which war?

Answers on page 90.

History 2

1 In which year was the Battle of Trafalgar?

2 What was the name of the first national political party of India founded in 1885?

3 The British Reform Act of 1884 extended the right to vote to whom?

4 In 1890 Luxembourg gained its independence from which country?

5 Who led the Labour Party to victory in the 1945 General Election?

6 Which president doubled the area of the USA by the purchase of the Louisiana Territory from the French in 1803?

7 Who became the first tsar of Russia in 1547?

8 In which year was the Berlin Wall opened, reuniting East and West Berlin?

9 Where was Napoleon exiled to following his defeat at the Battle of Waterloo in 1815?

10 Who was the longest-serving president of the USA?

Answers on page 90.

History 3

1 Who was the first Archbishop of Canterbury?

2 Which nineteenth-century German statesman was known as the Iron Chancellor?

3 Who became queen of England on the death of Edward VI in 1553?

4 What was the name of the London theatre where Shakespeare's plays were performed?

5 In which year did Guy Fawkes' Gunpowder Plot to blow up the Houses of Parliament take place?

6 Which battle began the English Civil War?

7 Which Englishman founded the American state of Pennsylvania in 1683?

8 Who became king and queen of England on the enforced abdication of James II in 1788?

9 Who was the British prime minister at the outbreak of the Napoleonic Wars in 1793?

10 Who led the first expedition to cross the Antarctic Circle?

Answers on page 91.

The Living World 1

1 The wobbegong, dogfish and hammerhead are all types of what?

2 Which plant, growing only in the Seychelles, produces the largest nut in the world?

3 How many legs does a lobster have?

4 What is a pinniped?

5 A clementine is a cross between which two fruits?

6 What type of creature is a pipistrelle?

7 What is the only bird species to have nostrils on its beak?

8 Which bird has the largest wing span?

9 Gamay, Grenache and Pinot Noir are all varieties of which fruit?

10 What type of animal is a Suffolk punch?

Answers on page 91.

The Living World 2

1 Which bird, sacred to the Ancient Mayas and Aztecs, is the national emblem of Guatemala?

2 What type of creature is an impala?

3 From which species of whale is ambergris, used in the manufacture of perfumes, obtained?

4 What is the common name of the plant whose Latin name is *Monstera deliciosa*?

5 What is a male horse aged under four called?

6 What is the fibre on a coconut called?

7 What is the fruit of the baobab tree of Africa and Australia called?

8 To what bird family does the kookaburra belong?

9 What type of creature is a widgeon?

10 If a creature is arboreal, where does it make its home?

Answers on page 91.

The Living World 3

1 What is the smallest European bird?

2 What is the common name of the plant whose Latin name is *Ficus elastica*?

3 What is a zoophyte?

4 By what process do plants capture and use energy from sunlight?

5 Leghorn, Rhode Island Red and Plymouth Rock are all breeds of what?

6 What type of creature is a titmouse?

7 From which animal does ermine fur come?

8 The fruit of which plant was once commonly known as love apples?

9 What is the name of the species of whale whose males have one long spiral tusk?

10 What type of creature is an ibex?

Answers on page 91.

Science and Technology 1

1 What is the substance in blood which causes clotting?

2 What is a prosthetic?

3 Which planet was discovered by William Herschel in 1781?

4 What is the medical term for the shoulder blades?

5 Name the physicist who first split the atom in 1919.

6 What is the name of the tube which connects the kidneys to the bladder?

7 What is France's high-speed passenger train called?

8 What gas is the Sun's core made of?

9 What pigment is naturally produced by the skin to protect it from the Sun's ultraviolet rays?

10 By what name is the viral infection rubeola better known?

Answers on page 91.

Science and Technology 2

1 By what name is the drug acetylsalicylic acid better known?

2 What is a nine-sided figure called?

3 What was unique about Louise Brown at the time of her birth in 1978?

4 What was the first animal in space?

5 What is the common name for the patella bone?

6 In the world of aviation what is STOL an abbreviation of?

7 How many blood groups are there?

8 What name is given to the mark on the side of a ship which shows the limit of legal submersion under various conditions?

9 Excluding the Sun, what is the nearest star to Earth?

10 What name is given to the watery substance which surrounds a growing foetus in the womb?

Answers on page 91.

Science and Technology 3

1. Where on the human body can the gluteus maximus be found?
2. The Bacille Calmette-Guérin or BCG vaccine protects against which illness?
3. What is the name of the alternative therapy which combines massage with the application of essential oils?
4. On the periodic table, which chemical element is classified as Mg?
5. The world's largest computer firm is IBM. What does IBM stand for?
6. Red blood cells contain a substance which is responsible for carrying oxygen in the blood. What is it called?
7. What is the layer of gas surrounding the Sun called?
8. Which three colours are called 'the primary colours of light'?
9. By what name is the condition of Daltonism more commonly known?
10. Who built the first steam train in 1804?

Answers on page 91.

Sports 1

1 From which country does Ajax football club come?

1 Who, in 1991, finally broke the long-standing longjump record which had been set by Bob Beamon?

3 In which year did women compete for the first time in an Olympic marathon?

4 In showjumping, how many faults are incurred for a fall?

5 What is the name of the yacht race which covers a distance of about 200 miles from Cowes on the Isle of Wight, to Fastnet Rock, Ireland, to Plymouth?

6 How many events are there in the heptathlon?

7 By what name is the sport of moto-cross also known?

8 Who was the first cricketer to score more than 2,000 runs in a single season?

9 With which team did British footballer Stanley Matthews, the 'wizard of the dribble', start his career?

10 With whom did Jimmy Connors team up to win the Men's Doubles tennis championship at Wimbledon in 1973?

Answers on page 91.

Sports 2

1 From which country does Juventus football club come?

2 In Olympic fencing, men can compete using each type of sword – the sabre, the foil and the epée – while women may use only one. Which?

3 What was the name of the English footballer who scored a hat-trick in the final of the 1966 World Cup?

4 In ten-pin bowling if all the pins are knocked down with one ball, it is called a strike; what is it called if two balls are taken to achieve this?

5 In which field event does athlete Sergey Bubka excel?

6 Where is the Oaks horse race held?

7 In American football how many points are awarded for a touchdown?

8 What is the name of the football ground at which Fulham football team is based?

9 In a basketball team, how many players can be on the court at any one time?

10 The Venus Rosewater Dish is presented to the winner of which tennis championship?

Answers on page 92.

Sports 3

1 What distances are covered in the two walking events held at the Olympic Games?

2 How often is the Whitbread Round the World yacht race held?

3 Who was the longest-reigning world heavyweight boxing champion from 1937–49?

4 What is the largest horse-racing course in the United Kingdom?

5 What score is indicated when an umpire puts his hands in the air during a cricket match?

6 What is the value of the pink ball in snooker?

7 At what ground in France are international rugby union matches played?

8 What events make up the triathlon?

9 With which sport are the names of Geoff Hunt, Jahangir Khan and Heather McKay associated?

10 How many lanes are there in an Olympic swimming pool?

Answers on page 92.

The Hot Spot

Art and Literature

1 What is the name of the pop artist famous for his comic-strip paintings such as *Whaam!*?

2 What is the name of the gang leader in Graham Greene's *Brighton Rock*?

3 What type of creature is Rikki-Tikki Tavi in Rudyard Kipling's *The Jungle Book*?

4 What was the name of the architect who designed the dome of Florence Cathedral?

5 Which four US presidents are immortalised in Gutzon Borglum's Mount Rushmore Memorial called simply *Presidents*?

6 What is the name of the storyteller in *The Arabian Nights* who begins a different story each night to prevent her execution?

7 What is the name of the count in Alexandre Dumas's novel *The Count of Monte Cristo*?

8 Which opera by Verdi is based on Alexandre Dumas's novel *The Lady of the Camelias*?

9 In Tennessee Williams's play *The Glass Menagerie*, what is the name of the central family?

10 In Edward Lear's nonsense poem 'The Owl and the Pussycat', who marries the unlikely pair?

Answers on page 92.

Film and TV

1 Which actor and actress played the parts of the mis-matched lovers in the 1961 film *Splendor in the Grass*?

2 Who wrote the novel on which Steven Spielberg's 1975 film thriller *Jaws* was based?

3 In the 1931 film *The Public Enemy* James Cagney pushed a grapefruit into the face of which actress?

4 What is the name of the science fiction novel on which Ridley Scott's 1983 film *Blade Runner*, starring Harrison Ford, is based?

5 For which company did the character played by Leonard Rossiter work in the television comedy series *The Fall and Rise of Reginald Perrin*?

6 In the television drama series *Rock Follies*, what was the name of the rock group formed by the three central female characters?

7 On the life of which composer was the 1945 film *A Song to Remember* based?

8 What was the name of the character played by Yul Brynner in *The King and I*?

9 What were the Christian names of the Cartwright brothers on *Bonanza*?

10 In the television science fiction series *Dr Who*, what does the acronym TARDIS stand for?

Answers on page 92.

Geography

1 In which European city can the Doge's Palace be found?

2 What is the name of the waterway that links the Baltic and the North Sea?

3 In which Indian city can the Taj Mahal be found?

4 What is the capital of Madagascar?

5 Name the world's longest traffic tunnel which links the Japanese islands of Hokkaido and Honshu.

6 What is the Welsh village whose name in English means: 'The Church of St Mary in a hollow of white hazel, near the rapid whirlpool and to St Tysilio Church, near to a red cave'.

7 Of which country is Godthaab the capital?

8 Where are the Taurus Mountains?

9 Grenada, St Lucia and Martinique belong to which group of islands?

10 What is the name of the Welsh village designed by architect Clough Williams Ellis, based on the town of Portofino in Italy?

Answers on page 92.

History

1 In Nazi Germany what was SS an abbreviation of?

2 Who was the first person to fly solo round the world in his plane *Winnie Mae* in 1933?

3 In which year was slavery abolished in Great Britain and her dependencies?

4 Under which English king was the Model Parliament called, forming the basis of the House of Commons?

5 What was the first permanent English settlement in North America, established in 1607?

6 What name did Dutch explorer Abel Tasman give to the island of Tasmania when he first landed there in 1642?

7 Which battle of 1890 marked the last Indian uprising in the USA?

8 The USA was the first country of the New World to claim its independence; which country in 1804 became the second to do so?

9 Who secured independence from Spain for Colombia, Venezuela, Peru and Bolivia during the years 1819–25?

10 Where was the first skyscraper built in 1883?

Answers on page 92.

The Living World

1 What type of creature is an ouzel?

2 Originally called a camelopard, by what name is this animal better known today?

3 In which part of a flower is the pollen contained?

4 What is a dhole?

5 What type of creature is an axolotl?

6 What spice is obtained from the *Curcuma longa* plant?

7 What type of creature is a gharial?

8 Which bird has claws on its wing tips?

9 Which plant, growing in the forests of south-east Asia, has the largest flowers?

10 Which island did the dodo inhabit?

Answers on page 92.

Science and Technology

1 What is the condition called where a constant noise can be heard in the ears?

2 What are Neptune's two moons called?

3 How many astronauts in all have landed on the Moon?

4 What is ethology the study of?

5 What is the classification for silver on the periodic table?

6 Who discovered radioactivity?

7 Who in 1834 drew up the first plans for a programmable digital computer, the Difference Engine?

8 What does the acronym for the computer language COBOL stand for?

9 What is the name for a parallelogram which has sides of an equal length?

10 Bones are covered by a thin skin that contains the cells which grow and divide to make new bone. What is this skin called?

Answers on page 93.

Sports

1 How many times did Sugar Ray Robinson hold the title world middleweight boxing champion?

2 Which sport has the largest pitch?

3 How big is the circle from which an athlete hurls the discus?

4 Where is France's most famous horse race, the Prix de l'Arc de Triomphe, held?

5 At which venue are the French tennis championships held?

6 In which sport is the Cy Young award given annually?

7 In athletics women do not participate in three field events. What are they?

8 What is the reserve crew of the Oxford rowing team called?

9 In 1971 the Wimbledon Mixed Doubles Championships were won by a brother and sister. Who were they?

10 With which sport are the names of Wilt Chamberlain, Kareem Adul-jabbar and Bill Russell associated?

Answers on page 93.

Round Three

TRUE OR FALSE?

In this final round, there are ten statements given in each quiz, five of which are true and five false. You must decide which are fact and which are fiction, but you have only 90 seconds in which to decide.

How to score: Score one point for each statement correctly identified as true or false. If you get all ten correct, award yourself five bonus points.

For added interest: Decide before you begin each quiz how many statements you will correctly categorise as true or false, starting with a minimum of five, and score as follows:

Five = 5 points; six = 10 points; seven = 15 points;
eight = 20 points; nine = 25 points; ten = 30 points.

But fail to identify correctly the number you have nominated and pay the hot spot penalty – no points for the quiz at all!

The final quiz in this section, Race to the Finish, makes an ideal final if more than one person is playing.

First Timers

1 On 18 January, 1912, Captain Robert Falcon Scott became the first person to reach the South Pole.

2 The first living creatures to fly in a hot air balloon were a duck, a sheep and a rooster.

3 The first motorways were built in Italy in the Twenties.

4 The USA was the first country to give women the vote.

5 Russian cosmonaut Yuri Gagarin was the first man to walk in space.

6 Ceylon (now Sri Lanka) became the first country to elect a woman as its prime minister in 1960.

7 Joshua Slocum was the first person to sail around the world single-handed, completing his journey in 1898.

8 Omega is the first letter of the Greek alphabet.

9 The first British television programme for children was *Watch with Mother*?

10 The cotton wedding anniversary is celebrated after the first year of marriage.

Answers on page 93.

Motor Racing Madness

1 The first major motor race run in the British Isles was the Gordon Bennett Trophy of 1903.

2 In the Le Mans motor race, no driver is allowed to drive for more than fourteen hours in a stint.

3 The worst motor racing accident occurred at Manza in 1928 when racing driver Materassi crashed his Talbot into the crowd, killing 23 people.

4 Silverstone racing circuit is built on an old airfield once used for RAF training.

5 In 1968, Graham Hill became the first British racing driver to win the World Championship.

6 British Grand Prix races are always held at Brands Hatch.

7 The first permanent racing driving school was established by Jim Russell at Snetterton in 1957.

8 The 1000 Lakes motor rally takes place in the country of Finland.

9 World Champion driver James Hunt raced for the Lotus team.

10 Before making his mark in the world of motor racing, Emerson Fittipaldi had been national kart-racing champion of Brazil.

Answers on page 93.

A Sporting Chance

1 In motor racing if a driver is disqualified a red flag is shown.

2 The sport of cricket was begun in Saxon times by shepherds. It derives its name from the word crook, which was used as the bat.

3 A bull-fighter's cloak is red.

4 In 1457 King James II of Scotland banned the playing of golf.

5 The Stanley Cup is competed for in the sport of ice hockey.

6 Henry Cooper is the only British boxer to have held the title World Heavyweight Champion.

7 The martial art of tae kwon do originates from Japan.

8 Octopush is the name of the unusual sport of underwater hockey, played between two teams of six players equipped with masks, fins, snorkels and small wooden or plastic spatulas.

9 The Olympic Games were last held in England in 1966.

10 The official frog jumping championships are held annually in Calveras, California.

Answers on page 93.

Lucky Dip

1 Penguins swim in the Arctic Ocean.

2 The Queen always faces right on stamps and coins.

3 The saffron spice comes from the crocus.

4 *The Laughing Cavalier* was painted by Rembrandt.

5 Tempera is a paint which includes egg yolk in its make up.

6 Bulldogs were originally bred to bait bulls.

7 The zodiac sign of Capricorn is symbolised by a ram.

8 The headquarters of the Open University are in Oxford.

9 In the Christian calendar the Epiphany is celebrated on 6 January.

10 The tulip originates from Turkey.

Answers on page 94.

Amazing Animals

1 A mouse's heart beats about 500 times a minute.

2 Nabokov's Pug is a species of butterfly named after its discoverer, author Vladimir Nabokov.

3 Bombay-duck is a small water fowl which nests along the River Ganges. It is caught by local fishermen who salt, dry and sell it for export as a delicacy.

4 Zoophobia is a fear of animals.

5 A slow worm is a type of lizard.

6 Borzoi, papillon and Saluki are all types of butterfly.

7 A horse's withers are found at the back of its calves.

8 The blue whale, the world's largest creature, has the biggest eye in the animal kingdom, measuring about the size of a large dinner plate.

9 The hyrax, a small furry animal about the size of a guinea pig, is the elephant's only living relative.

10 Sharks have a swim bladder to help maintain buoyancy in the water.

Answers on page 94.

Tall Stories

1 Before he became a professional writer, novelist Dick Francis was a jockey.

2 William Shakespeare was the first poet laureate.

3 The Prince of Wales wrote *The Old Man of Lochnagar*.

4 Ian Fleming, creator of James Bond, wrote the story on which the film *Chitty Chitty Bang Bang* was based.

5 In Charles Dickens's novel *A Tale of Two Cities* the action is set in London and Florence.

6 Novelist Anthony Trollope was responsible for introducing the pillar-box into Great Britain.

7 British novelist Joseph Conrad could not speak English until he was 19 years old.

8 *Portrait of the Artist as a Young Dog* was written by James Joyce.

9 The leader of the animals in George Orwell's *Animal Farm* was a carthorse.

10 First World War poet, naval officer Rupert Brooke was killed in action in the Dardanelles.

Answers on page 94.

The Big Screen

1 In the 1963 version of *Cleopatra*, Rex Harrison played Anthony to Elizabeth Taylor's Cleopatra.

2 Walt Disney was the first person to provide a voice for his much-loved mouse character.

3 British actor Stewart Granger's real name was James Stewart.

4 In the 1985 thriller *Witness*, starring Harrison Ford and Kelly McGillis, the action was set within a community of Mormons.

5 In *Angels with Dirty Faces* gangster Rocky Sullivan, played by James Cagney, was gunned down in a restaurant by a rival gang.

6 All the actors in Derek Jarman's 1976 film *Sebastiane* spoke only in Latin.

7 Akira Kurosawa's 1957 film *Throne of Blood* is based on Shakespeare's *King Lear*.

8 In Walt Disney's animated film *Peter Pan* the character of Tinkerbell was modelled on Marilyn Monroe.

9 The 1945 film *Brief Encounter*, directed by David Lean and starring Trevor Howard and Celia Johnson, was based on Noel Coward's stageplay *Still Lives*.

10 Sylvester Stallone played the part of *Conan the Barbarian* in the 1982 film of the same name.

Answers on page 94.

Hard to Place

1. The Pacific Ocean is bigger than the total land area of the Earth.
2. New York is the capital of the USA.
3. Sudd is the name given to an area of swamp in Sudan.
4. Texas is the largest state in the USA.
5. The Angel Falls in Venezuela were named after US adventurer Jimmy Angel.
6. The Trans-Siberian railway line is the world's longest.
7. A Beefeater is a guard at the Houses of Parliament.
8. The Uffizi art gallery can be found in Milan, Italy.
9. Rio de Janeiro is the capital of Brazil.
10. The country of Indonesia is made up of over 13,000 islands.

Answers on page 94.

Wonderful Human Beings

1. The stirrup bone can be found at the back of the foot.
2. The most common eye colour is blue.
3. Skin cells only last about one week before they die.
4. If all the blood vessels in the human body were joined together they could stretch around the world two and a half times.
5. The function of red blood cells is to fight infection.
6. Tears are produced by the lacrymal glands.
7. About one in every 1000 births in Britain results in twins.
8. A rhinologist specialises in the treatment of the nose.
9. A baby cannot blush.
10. Edward Jenner discovered that blood circulates around the body.

Answers on page 94.

Fantastic Food

1 Brown eggs are better for you than white ones.

2 The Mexican dish of guacamole is made from avocados.

3 Black velvet is a cocktail produced by mixing stout and champagne.

4 A teaspoon of ground coffee contains more caffeine than a teaspoon of tea leaves.

5 Tapas are Mexican stuffed pancakes.

6 Spinach, Popeye the sailorman's favourite food, has about ten times as much iron content as any other vegetable.

7 Joseph Priestley, co-discoverer of oxygen, invented the first fizzy drink.

8 Fugu is a Japanese delicacy, prepared by specially licensed chefs, from the puffer or flowfish, the world's most poisonous fish.

9 The words extra-sec on a champagne label mean the wine is very sweet.

10 Sherry gets its name from its place of origin – Jerez in Spain.

Answers on page 95.

Race to the Finish

1 Lapidary is the craft of cutting and polishing gems.

2 Gainsborough painted the ceiling of the Banqueting Hall in London's Whitehall.

3 An amphora is a Greek vase or storage jar.

4 The Albert Memorial can be found in London's Hyde Park.

5 Rutland is the United Kingdom's smallest county.

6 Boy George played in the group Bow, Wow, Wow.

7 Realtor is the American term for an estate agent.

8 Coronations of British monarchs always take place in St Paul's Cathedral.

9 The world's most spoken language is English.

10 The griffin is a mythical creature which has the head of an eagle and the body of a lion.

Answers on page 95.

ANSWERS

ROUND ONE: MATCH-UPS

Star Turns
1E; 2I; 3B; 4G; 5H; 6J; 7C; 8A; 9D; 10F.

Cities of the World
1H; 2D; 3F; 4A; 5J; 6B; 7I; 8C; 9E; 10G.

An Inventive Mind
1F; 2I; 3J; 4G; 5A; 6H; 7C; 8D; 9E; 10B.

In Which Year? A Time of Peace
1F; 2G; 3J; 4B; 5H; 6A; 7I; 8D; 9C; 10E.

Don't Be Afraid
1G; 2D; 3F; 4H; 5J; 6I; 7C; 8E; 9A; 10B.

Ten Detectives in Search of an Author
1H; 2E; 3A; 4G; 5I; 6D; 7B; 8J; 9C; 10F.

God Save Them
1H; 2G; 3D; 4A; 5E; 6C; 7J; 8I; 9B; 10F.

Sporting Winners
1J; 2E; 3G; 4F; 5C; 6H; 7I; 8D; 9B; 10A.

Philosophically Speaking
1E; 2I; 3G; 4H; 5B; 6J; 7D; 8A; 9F; 10C.

In Which Year? Fifties/Sixties
1E; 2H; 3J; 4A; 5F; 6B; 7I; 8D; 9C; 10G.

Beat the Bard
1C; 2H; 3G; 4F; 5B; 6I; 7J; 8E; 9A; 10D.

Famous Last Words
1E; 2G; 3H; 4B; 5I; 6C; 7D; 8J; 9A; 10F.

Out of Africa
1H; 2E; 3G; 4F; 5A; 6I; 7C; 8J; 9B; 10D.

Pen Names
1E; 2I; 3G; 4F; 5C; 6A; 7J; 8B; 9D; 10H.

Legendary Figures
1H; 2F; 3G; 4A; 5I; 6B; 7J; 8D; 9E; 10C.

Singalong Time
1D; 2J; 3I; 4H; 5F; 6C; 7B; 8E; 9A; 10G.

In Which Year? Seventies/Eighties
1J; 2F; 3H; 4A; 5I; 6B; 7E; 8C; 9G; 10D.

Childhood Classics
1F; 2G; 3E; 4H; 5I; 6J; 7B; 8D; 9A; 10C.

Politically Speaking
1C; 2F; 3A; 4I; 5G; 6D; 7J; 8E; 9H; 10B.

Star Turns Take Two
1C; 2D; 3I; 4G; 5H; 6J; 7B; 8A; 9E; 10F.

The Day Job
1G; 2J; 3E; 4H; 5I; 6B; 7D; 8C; 9F; 10A.

Olympic Winners
1H; 2J; 3A; 4F; 5B; 6I; 7D; 8E; 9G; 10C.

States of the USA
1E; 2F; 3J; 4H; 5G; 6I; 7A; 8B; 9C; 10D.

Collectively Speaking
1D; 2H; 3G; 4I; 5J; 6A; 7E; 8B; 9C; 10F.

Zzzzzzzz!
1H; 2E; 3G; 4B; 5J; 6C; 7I; 8F; 9A; 10D.

ROUND ONE: KNOWLEDGE TESTERS

Easy Starters

Art and Literature 1

1 Belgian **2** Mary Shelley. **3** Henry VIII. **4** Hans Christian Andersen. **5** 'Minute Waltz'. **6** Botticelli. **7** Evelyn Waugh. **8** Switzerland. **9** L.S. Lowry. **10** George Gershwin.

Art and Literature 2

1 John, Michael and Wendy. **2** The Napoleonic Wars. **3** *The Ring of the Nibelung.* **4** Anna Sewell. **5** Sir Christopher Wren. **6** Willy Wonka. **7** Iris Murdoch. **8** Charlotte. **9** Toulouse-Lautrec. **10** Bob Cratchit.

Art and Literature 3

1 F. Scott Fitzgerald. **2** *Metamorphosis.* **3** Titania. **4** Paddington. **5** *Great Expectations.* **6** Constable. **7** Virgil. **8** Lord Byron. **9** Dr Seuss. **10** H.G. Wells.

Film and TV 1

1 Una Stubbs. **2** *Carry on Columbus.* **3** Norman Bates. **4** Huey, Dewey and Louie. **5** *Shampoo.* **6** *Dynasty.* **7** *The Sound of Music.* **8** *Give Us a Clue.* **9** Marlene Dietrich. **10** Mary Whitehouse.

Film and TV 2

1 Humphrey Bogart. **2** *Star Wars.* **3** The Woolpack. **4** Raymond Chandler. **5** James Stewart. **6** *Alias Smith and Jones.* **7** Janet Leigh and Tony Curtis. **8** *Rainbow.* **9** Magnus Magnusson. **10** Julie Walters and Michael Caine.

Film and TV 3

1 Mortimer. **2** Charles Bronson. **3** Bet Gilroy (née Lynch). **4** Damien. **5** Grace Brothers. **6** Alan Bleasdale. **7** Robert de Niro. **8** *The Avengers.* **9** Gerry and Sylvia Anderson. **10** *In Sickness and in Health.*

Geography 1

1 Rhodesia. **2** Organisation of Petroleum Exporting Countries. **3** The Yellow River. **4** Austria and Switzerland. **5** Oslo. **6** Grand Union Canal. **7** Red Sea and the Mediterranean. **8** Crete. **9** French. **10** Rio de Janeiro.

Geography 2
1 Youth hostel. **2** The Pennines. **3** Pacific Ocean. **4** Mont Blanc. **5** Serpentine. **6** Vienna. **7** Birmingham. **8** Iran. **9** The State of the Vatican City in Rome, Italy. **10** Yen.

Geography 3
1 Denmark. **2** Gaucho. **3** France and Spain. **4** Houses of Parliament. **5** Switzerland. **6** Cairo. **7** The Solent. **8** The Great Lakes. **9** A geyser. **10** The Tay.

History 1
1 *Hindenberg.* **2** John Wilkes Booth. **3** Conquistadores. **4** Battle of Hastings (1066). **5** Neil Armstrong. **6** The Hundred Years' War. **7** Henry VIII. **8** One penny (the Penny Black). **9** Joseph Stalin. **10** 1939.

History 2
1 Richard Nixon. **2** Charles Darwin. **3** Alcohol. **4** Nuremberg. **5** Fourth of July, 1776. **6** Emily Pankhurst. **7** The Huns. **8** War of the Roses. **9** Ming Dynasty. **10** James I.

History 3
1 1666. **2** Nazis. **3** Tolpuddle Martyrs. **4** Edward VII. **5** World War I (1914–18). **6** League of Nations. **7** Donald Campbell. **8** Runnymeade. **9** She was guillotined. **10** *Mayflower.*

The Living World 1
1 Ostrich. **2** Omnivore. **3** Giant panda. **4** Old man's beard. **5** Monkey. **6** Emperor penguin. **7** Apple. **8** Mallard. **9** Dock: **10** Pig.

The Living World 2
1 They are flightless. **2** An amphibian. **3** Butterfly. **4** Fuchsia. **5** Elf owl. **6** Fish. **7** Coca plant. **8** Arachnids. **9** The potato. **10** Vixen.

The Living World 3
1 Great auk. **2** Sheep. **3** Holly. **4** Chihuahua. **5** Melon. **6** Lizard. **7** Three. **8** On its tail. **9** Willow. **10** Koala bear.

Science and Technology 1
1 Soft spots. **2** The heel. **3** Yuri Gagarin. **4** Fossils. **5** Chickenpox. **6** Six. **7** Eyes. **8** Nine. **9** Diamond. **10** Radiographer.

Science and Technology 2
1 Kidneys. **2** The Boeing 747 or Jumbo Jet. **3** Aqueduct. **4** Vertebrae. **5** Air, fire, water and earth. **6** Paediatrician. **7** *Salyut 1*. **8** Brain. **9** Haemophilia. **10** Eight.

Science and Technology 3
1 Astronomers. **2** The femur or thigh bone. **3** AIDS. **4** Feet. **5** Jupiter. **6** Gliders. **7** Black holes. **8** Acupuncture. **9** A mouse. **10** Mars.

Sports 1
1 Cassius Clay. **2** Ibrox Park. **3** Roger Bannister. **4** Pelé. **5** 1966. **6** Twenty-four hours. **7** Orienteering. **8** Snooker. **9** Javelin. **10** Chelsea.

Sports 2
1 Austrian. **2** High jump. **3** Golf. **4** Isle of Man. **5** Norwich City. **6** American Football. **7** Liverpool. **8** Boxing. **9** Sixty. **10** June.

Sports 3
1 Tottenham Hotspur. **2** Basketball. **3** Albertville, France. **4** Showjumping. **5** Southampton. **6** Boxing. **7** Twickenham. **8** Cricket. **9** Whist. **10** Hockey.

Warming Up

Art and Literature 1
1 Fauvism. **2** *Old Possum's Book of Practical Cats.* **3** James Boswell. **4** *Dr Doolittle* by Hugh Lofting. **5** Dario Fo. **6** Bizet. **7** Publican. **8** Margaret Mitchell. **9** Caliban. **10** Yukio Mishima.

Art and Literature 2
1 Bill Sikes. **2** *Claudius the God.* **3** Rodin. **4** Benjamin Britten. **5** Passepartout. **6** Malcolm Bradbury. **7** Amy, Beth, Jo and Meg March. **8** *Rosencrantz and Guildenstern are Dead.* **9** Pemberton. **10** *The Catcher in the Rye.*

Art and Literature 3
1 *The Loneliness of the Long-Distance Runner.* **2** Betsy Trotwood. **3** Jack Kerouac. **4** *Whistler's Mother.* **5** University lecturer. **6** J.S. Bach. **7** Cholera. **8** Manderley. **9** Luigi Pirandello. **10** Daniel Defoe.

Film and TV 1

1 *Apocalypse Now.* **2** Audrey Hepburn. **3** Bluto. **4** *The Mary Tyler Moore Show.* **5** Ridley Scott. **6** *The Prime of Miss Jean Brodie.* **7** Lord Reith. **8** L. Frank Baum. **9** Ena Sharples. **10** Harry Lime.

Film and TV 2

1 Mrs Robinson. **2** *Reach for the Sky.* **3** Wendy Craig. **4** *Dead Ringers.* **5** Betty Boop. **6** The Vietnam War. **7** Lurch. **8** Bob Monkhouse - they have all been presented by him. **9** *The Coalminer's Daughter.* **10** Venice.

Film and TV 3

1 Jerry and Margot Leadbetter. **2** Ian Ogilvy. **3** James Mason. **4** King's Oak. **5** It was a leopard. **6** St Eligius. **7** Dolly Parton. **8** Peter Fluck and Roger Law. **9** Arthur Fonzerelli. **10** Richard Harris.

Geography 1

1 Thailand. **2** Brazzaville. **3** Colorado River. **4** Balearic Islands. **5** At the southern tip of South America. **6** Northernmost: Reykjavik (Iceland). Southernmost: Wellington (New Zealand). **7** Sofia. **8** Amstel. **9** Damascus. **10** Sacramento.

Geography 2

1 The lotus flower. **2** Belgium. **3** Valetta. **4** Cook Strait. **5** Algeria. **6** The Po. **7** Somerset. **8** The city of Luxembourg. **9** Argentina, Brazil and Bolivia. **10** Cambridge.

Geography 3

1 Hong Kong. **2** Jamaica. **3** A hill created by a glacier. **4** India and Burma. **5** The Arno. **6** Copenhagen. **7** Sri Lanka. **8** Isthmus. **9** Lagos. **10** The Occident.

History 1

1 The Sun God, Helios. **2** Jefferson Davis. **3** Lady Nancy Astor. **4** Bay of Pigs. **5** Henry VII. **6** The Thirty Years War. **7** Martin Luther. **8** 1642. **9** George Washington. **10** Crimean War (1854-56).

History 2

1 1805. **2** Indian National Congress. **3** All males over the age of 21. **4** Holland. **5** Attlee. **6** Thomas Jefferson. **7** Ivan IV (The Terrible). **8** 1989. **9** St Helena. **10** Franklin D. Roosevelt.

History 3
1 Saint Augustine. **2** Otto Eduard Leopold von Bismarck. **3** Mary I. **4** Globe Theatre. **5** 1605. **6** Battle of Edgehill. **7** William penn. **8** William III and Mary II. **9** William Pitt the Younger. **10** Captain James Cook.

The Living World 1
1 Sharks. **2** The coco-de-mer. **3** Ten. **4** A mammal with flippers, i.e. walrus, seal and sea-lion. **5** An orange and a tangerine. **6** Bat. **7** Kiwi. **8** Albatross. **9** The grape. **10** A carthorse.

The Living World 2
1 Quetzal. **2** Antelope. **3** Sperm whale. **4** Swiss cheese plant. **5** Colt. **6** Coir. **7** Monkey bread. **8** Kingfisher. **9** Duck. **10** In the trees.

The Living World 3
1 The goldcrest. **2** Rubber plant. **3** Any animal resembling a plant, e.g. sea anemone. **4** Photosynthesis. **5** Chicken. **6** Bird. **7** Stoat. **8** Tomato. **9** Narwhal. **10** Goat.

Science and Technology 1
1 Fibrin. **2** An artificial body part. **3** Uranus. **4** Scapulae. **5** Ernest Rutherford. **6** Ureter. **7** Train à Grande Vitesse. **8** Helium. **9** Melanin. **10** Measles.

Science and Technology 2
1 Aspirin. **2** Nonagon. **3** She was the first test-tube baby. **4** Dog. **5** Knee cap. **6** Short Take Off and Landing. **7** Four – A, B, AB, and O. **8** The Plimsoll line. **9** Proxima Centauri. **10** Amniotic fluid.

Science and Technology 3
1 Buttocks. **2** Tuberculosis Bacillus or TB. **3** Aromatherapy. **4** Magnesium. **5** International Business Machines. **6** Haemoglobin. **7** Chromosphere. **8** Red, green and blue. **9** Colour blindness. **10** Richard Trevithick.

Sports 1
1 Netherlands. **2** Mike Powell. **3** 1984. **4** Eight. **5** Admiral's Cup. **6** Seven. **7** Scrambling. **8** W.G. Grace. **9** Stoke City Football Club. **10** Ilie Nastase.

Sports 2

1 Italy. **2** The foil. **3** Geoff Hurst. **4** A spare. **5** Pole vault. **6** Epsom Downs, Surrey. **7** Six. **8** Craven Cottage. **9** Five. **10** Wimbledon's Women's Singles Championship.

Sports 3

1 Twenty kilometres and 50 km. **2** Every four years. **3** Joe Louis. **4** Newmarket. **5** Six runs. **6** Six. **7** Parc des Princes. **8** Swimming (3.8 km), Cycling (180 km) and the Marathon. **9** Squash. **10** Eight.

The Hot Spot

Art and Literature

1 Roy Lichtenstein. **2** Pinkie Brown. **3** Mongoose. **4** Brunelleschi. **5** George Washington, Thomas Jefferson, Abraham Lincoln and Theodore Roosevelt. **6** Scheherezade. **7** Edmond Dantes. **8** *La Traviata.* **9** Wingfields. **10** The turkey.

Film and TV

1 Natalie Wood and Warren Beatty. **2** Peter Benchley. **3** Mae Clarke. **4** *Do Androids Dream of Electric Sheep* by Philip K. Dick. **5** Sunshine Desserts. **6** The Little Ladies. **7** Chopin. **8** King Mong Kut, the King of Siam. **9** Adam, Hoss and Little Joe. **10** Time And Relative Dimensions In Space.

Geography

1 Venice, Italy. **2** Kiel Canal. **3** Agra. **4** Tananarive. **5** Seikan Tunnel. **6** Llanfairpwllgwyngyllgogerychwyrndrobwllllantysiliogogogogoch or Llanfair PG for short!. **7** Greenland. **8** Turkey. **9** Windward Islands. **10** Portmeirion.

History

1 Schutzstaffel. **2** US pilot Wiley Post. **3** 1834. **4** Edward I. **5** Jamestown, Virginia. **6** Van Dieman's Land. **7** The Battle of Wounded Knee. **8** Haiti. **9** Simón Bolívar. **10** Chicago: it had ten storeys.

The Living World

1 A bird. **2** Giraffe. **3** The anther in the stamen. **4** An Indian wild dog. **5** A salamander. **6** Turmeric. **7** Crocodile. **8** Hoatzin. **9** Rafflesia. **10** Mauritius.

Science and Technology
1 Tinnitus. **2** Triton and Nereid. **3** Twelve. **4** Human behaviour. **5** Ag. **6** Henri Becquerel. **7** Charles Babbage. **8** *Co*mmon *B*usiness *O*rientated *L*anguage. **9** Rhombus. **10** Periosteum.

Sports
1 Five. **2** Polo. **3** Two and a half metres. **4** Longchamp, Paris. **5** Stade Roland Garros, Paris. **6** Baseball (to the outstanding pitcher on the major leagues). **7** Hammer, pole vault and the triple jump. **8** Isis. **9** John and Tracy Austin (USA). **10** Basketball.

ROUND THREE: TRUE OR FALSE?

First Timers
1 False, he was beaten by Captain Roald Amundsen of Norway by about a month. **2** True, in 1783 they safely underwent an eight-minute journey in a balloon built by the Montgolfier brothers. **3** True. **4** False, New Zealand in 1893 was the first country to give women the vote. American women had to wait until 1920 before they had the right to vote. **5** False, Yuri Gagarin was the first man in space; the first man to spacewalk was Alexi Leonov in 1965. **6** True, her name was Mrs Sirimavo Bandaranaike. **7** True. **8** False, alpha is the first letter. **9** False, it was *For the Children.* **10** True.

Motor Racing Madness
1 True. **2** False, a driver cannot drive for more than four hours in a stint or 14 hours in total. **3** False, the worst motor racing accident occurred in 1955 during the Le Mans motor race when a Mercedes-Benz, driven by Pierre Levegh, ploughed into a public enclosure killing the driver and 83 spectators. **4** True. **5** False, it was Mike Hawthorn in 1958. **6** False, Silverstone is an alternate venue. **7** True. **8** True. **9** False, he raced for McLaren. **10** True.

A Sporting Chance
1 False, a black flag is shown. **2** True. **3** False, it is red one side and yellow the other. **4** True. **5** True, it is contested by the National Hockey League of North America. **6** False, the only British boxer to have held this title was Bob Fitzsimmons in 1897.

7 False, it comes from Korea. **8** True. **9** False, they were last held in London in 1948. **10** True.

Lucky Dip
1 False, they swim in the Antarctic Ocean. **2** False, she always faces left. **3** True. **4** False, Frans Hals painted it. **5** True. **6** True. **7** False, it is a goat. **8** False, they are in Milton Keynes. **9** True, it is also known as Twelfth Night. **10** True.

Amazing Animals
1 True. **2** True. **3** False, it is a small fish. **4** True. **5** True. **6** False, they are all dog breeds. **7** False, they are behind the neck between the shoulders. **8** False, the blue whale has a disproportionately small eye compared to its body size; the giant squid has the largest eye measuring 400 mm across. **9** True. **10** False, unlike most fish, sharks do not have a swim bladder; instead they use their pectoral fins to keep themselves afloat.

Tall Stories
1 True. **2** False, Ben Jonson was. **3** True. **4** True. **5** False, the two cities referred to in the novel's title are London and Paris. **6** True, in his capacity as a high-ranking civil servant in the Post Office. **7** True, he was born and raised in Poland. **8** False, the author was Dylan Thomas. **9** False, their leader was a pig called Napoleon. **10** False, he died of blood poisoning caused by a mosquito bite before he even reached the battleground.

The Big Screen
1 False, the part of Anthony was played by Richard Burton. **2** True, he was the voice artist on *Steamboat Willie* (1928). **3** True, he had to change it in the mid-Thirties to avoid confusion with the Hollywood star James Stewart. **4** False, it was an Amish religious community. **5** False, he died in the electric chair. **6** True. **7** False, it is based on *Macbeth.* **8** True. **9** True. **10** False, Arnold Schwarzenegger had the lead role.

Hard to Place
1 True. **2** False, it is Washington D.C. **3** True. **4** False, it is Alaska. **5** True. **6** True. **7** False, he is a guard at the Tower of London. **8** False, it is in Florence. **9** False, Brasilia replaced Rio as Brazil's capital in 1960. **10** True.

Wonderful Human Beings
1 False, it is in the ear. **2** False, it is brown. **3** True. **4** True. **5** False, they carry oxygen around the body; white blood cells fight

disease. **6** True. **7** False, one in every 80 births results in twins. **8** True. **9** True, it is a reflex action which develops between the ages of two and four. **10** False, William Harvey made this discovery. Edward Jenner was a pioneer of vaccination.

Food Fantastic

1 False, egg shell colour is merely a characteristic of the breed of chicken. **2** True. **3** True. **4** False, but tea has less effect on the body as generally it is much more diluted when used. **5** False, they are Spanish appetisers. The taco is a stuffed fried pancake. **6** False, this is a popular misconception caused by a misplaced decimal point in a set of food tables published in 1870. Generally, vegetables contain the same amount of iron. **7** True. **8** True. **9** False, it means very dry. **10** True.

Race to the Finish

1 True. **2** False, Rubens was the artist. **3** True. **4** False, it is situated in Kensington Gardens. **5** False, Rutland ceased to exist when county boundaries were changed in 1974 and it became part of Leicestershire. The Isle of Wight is now England's smallest county. **6** True. **7** True. **8** False, they are held in Westminster Abbey. **9** False, it is Mandarin. **10** True.